Glendalough

Gleann Dá Loch

"The Valley of the Two Lakes"

Also known as

"The Valley of the Seven Churches"

The Pilgrim's Guide

By Fr. Thaddeus Doyle

Publisher

'Glendalough - The Pilgrims Guide' is published by Fr. Thaddeus Doyle, Shillelagh, Arklow, Co. Wicklow, Ireland.

© Fr. Thaddeus Doyle 2010. Colour design: Martina Davis

ISBN 978-0-9560424-2-2

Contents

All **photographs** were taken during the snow of January 2010

P. 3 "The Valley of the Seven Churches"

P. 4 Coming to Glendalough as a pilgrim and the special chaplet.

P. 6 Visiting the ancient buildings in the Monastic City as a pilgrim.
  The Round Tower, the Cathedral, St. Kevin's Church, St. Ciaran's Church, and the Priests House.

P. 14 St. Mary's Church - the ladies church

P. 16 Going as a pilgrim to Reefert Church and St. Kevin's Cell.

P. 20 St. Kevin's bed and the Church on the rock.

P. 22 Trinity Church and St. Mochuarog.

P. 23 St. Lawrence O Toole and St. Saviour's Church.

P. 26 St. Kevin - his life.

P. 27 St. Kevin and the woman who tried to seduce him.

P. 28 How St. Kevin exorcised Glendalough.

P. 30 The destruction of Glendalough

P. 31 The Deerstone, Holy Wells, and other items of interest.

P. 34 Prayer Walking in Glendalough
  P. 35 Prayer Walk 1 - on the level
  P. 36 Praying as one climbs
  P. 37 Prayer Walk 2
  P. 39 Prayer Walk 3
  P. 40 Prayer Walk 4
  P. 43 Prayer Walk 5
  P. 44 Prayer Walk 6

P. 45 Having one's eternal spirit come alive deep within

P. 46 The Modern St. Kevin's Church, Glendalough.

P. 47 God's Cottage Prayer Centre, Glendalough

P. 48 Mass times, food, toilets, accommodation etc.

From left:- St. Kevin's Church, the top of the Round Tower, the ruins of the Cathedral, and in the bottom right corner, the foundations of St. Ciaran's Church.

"The Valley Of The Seven Churches"

There were at least nine churches in the valley, though not all at the same time. However seven was a symbolic number for most ancient religions - a symbol of totality. For Christians, God made the world in seven days. There are seven days in the week and seven sacraments. In the Old Testament prayer is to be repeated seven times or for seven days, see P. 33. Seven also became a symbol of the power of the 3 Divine Persons over the 4 cardinal points, North, South, East and West. So the title "The Valley of the Seven Churches" is a symbol that this is God's valley.

In the later centuries, the seven Churches clearly visible were St. Saviour's, a mile down the valley from the monastic city, Trinity Church a half mile down the valley, The Cathedral and St. Kevin's Church in the inner city, St. Mary's (the Ladies Church) in the outer monastic city, Reefert Church beside the Upper Lake close to St. Kevin's Cell, and Teampul na Skellig on a small man-levelled bank at the back of the Upper Lake.

The original phrase was however "The Seven Churches of St. Kevin". St. Saviour's founded by St. Laurence O Toole would likely not have been included. It is possible that Trinity Church, always reputed to have been founded by St. Mochuarog, a disciple of St. Kevin, would also have been omitted. The Church of St. Ciaran, the remains of which were unearthed in 1875, would have been on the list, and possibly also a second little Church near the Upper Lake, only the bare outline of which now remains.

Coming To Glendalough As A Pilgrim

In ancient times most pilgrims came walking over the mountains. Their pilgrimage formally started in Hollywood then known as Killinkeyvin a full 30 km away. They came praying. Seven pilgrimages to Glendalough were considered equal to one pilgrimage to Rome. Special prayer stations were erected for pilgrims to pray at along the way.

Today's pilgrim has the opportunity to pray at the different sacred sites.

The monastic sites are now owned by the Office of Public Works, while much of the surrounding countryside is a National Park. We are indebted to them for the way they have cared for the ancient buildings and for the way they have opened up the area to the public. Sadly, however, one isn't free to hold public ceremonies without special permission, but one does not need permission to pray quietly or to sit in meditation.

In ancient times people travelled from all over Europe to Glendalough as pilgrims. Today even greater numbers travel there, but most come only as tourists. Please help reclaim this valley for the Lord. As you visit the sacred sites, do so in a spirit of prayer as a pilgrim.

Lord Jesus, help me to be touched by and to reawaken your sacred presence in Glendalough. May your sacred presence touch and envelope every person who visits this valley.

The Special Glendalough Chaplet

For some 1,400 years, people have been coming to Glendalough as pilgrims, interceding for their intentions as they come. In my own thirty plus years of coming here as a pilgrim, I have developed my own method of praying there based on an adaption of the Chaplet of Mercy.

Start with the Our Father, Hail Mary and Creed. Then on the Our Father beads, pray the usual, **"Eternal Father I offer you the body and blood, soul and divinity of your dearly beloved Son, our Lord Jesus Christ in atonement for my sins and the sins of the whole world."**

On the Hail Mary beads, pray, **"For the sake of His sorrowful passion, and through the intercession of St. Kevin and all the saints of Glendalough ...** (either insert your own intention or use the usual words "have mercy on us and on the whole world").

Offer a decade at **five or possibly seven** of the sacred sites of your choice, or as you walk in the sacred place. Alternative wordings for the prayer on the Hail Mary beads are given inside for different sacred sites, but do not feel that you have to use them all or to say mental prayers at every spot. **Glendalough is about solitude; about being in the presence of the Lord, and of responding to the prayers that rise up naturally in your own spirit.**

Equip Yourself With A Beads For Praying On When Walking

Equip yourself with either a rosary ring, or a single decade beads, or a double decade beads. They are convenient when walking fast and when climbing mountains, and they are also discreet for praying with, when in the midst of crowds of tourists.
Get into the habit of having them in your fingers as you visit the sacred sites. Your mind will start tuning in to God when there is a beads on your finger. Even when one is not repeating formal prayers, the beads on one's finger helps the mind to be aware of the presence of God.

Entering The Holy City

Today one enters through a double arched gateway. It is the only surviving monastic entrance of its kind in Ireland. Over this entrance was the gatekeeper's residence. The complete structure was still standing in 1795. This was the official entrance when Glendalough became a place of eminence. But most of the original pilgrims came by the 'Pilgrims Path' over the mountains and down by the Upper Lake to Reefert Church.

Here, just inside on the right, there is a very large slab with a very basic cross etched into it. This slab is centuries older than the actual entrance. The cross etched into it marked the point of sanctuary. Anyone who entered beyond it had the protection of the monastic city. Sadly however there were those who had no respect for holy places, and the very city itself was repeatedly attacked and plundered.

Yet it is a reminder to us that inside this gateway is a holy place:- a place sanctified by the lives of those who totally dedicated themselves to God, and some who were martyred during the raids here. While the entrance is usually busy, try to have a sense of the sacred as you walk up the steps.

Lord Jesus, help me to open my heart to You in this sacred place. May my pilgrimage here bring blessing to myself and others.

Cathedral of St. Peter and Paul
(At a later stage also known as the Cathedral of the Sacred Heart)

With interior dimensions of 49 foot by 30 foot for the nave, and a generous 25 foot by 22 foot for the sanctuary, plus walls that are 3.5 foot thick, this was quite a building for the time, the centrepiece of the monastic city.

Originally built in stages, starting with the nave sometime around 900 AD, it was clearly rebuilt, while retaining the bottom of the walls with their large square stones, several times over the next six hundred years. The location of the cathedral, at the very heart of the monastic city, is an indication that the first cathedral on this spot was built very early on.

Here the main Mass for Glendalough was celebrated by bishops and saints, including St. Laurence O Toole. Go to the sanctuary area, and become aware of, even breathe in, all the times that the bread and wine were transformed into the body and blood of Jesus on this very spot.

Lord I unite myself with all the Masses offered here.
May Your Sacred Presence rise up and envelope me and envelope everyone who enters this cathedral.

Then pray for your own intentions, possibly walking around inside the cathedral. Possible alternative wording for a decade in Cathedral,

"For the sake of His sorrowful passion, and through the intercession of St. Kevin, St. Laurence and all the saints of Glendalough ...... (insert intention).

The High Cross

The High Cross was erected in the 600s as the focal point of both the graveyard and the Monastic City. It is several hundred years older than the present buildings in the monastic city.

It is very plain when compared with High Crosses in places like Clonmacnoise, but it is much older than them. Also cutting designs in granite using the basic tools of the time was not easy. This may explain why the circular section around the place of the head of Jesus wasn't perforated to make a 'halo'. This section is also quite small possibly to reduce the pressure of the wind given that it is not perforated.

Erecting the High Cross was an act of dedicating the monastic enclosure to God, and of placing their lives under the power of the cross. It was also the focal point of the graveyard.

Over the centuries a silly myth grew up that there is blessing for those who can wrap their arms around it behind their backs. Due to the many tourists crowding around it to wrap their arms around the cross, it may be difficult to pray a decade here.

Instead as you touch it, or touch your beads to it, or just pray in its vicinity, entrust your life to God, possibly using words like these,

"For the sake of His sorrowful passion, and through the intercession of St. Kevin and of all the saints of Glendalough, I dedicate to You all that I am and all that I have."

The Priests' House with St. Mary's Church in the background.

Remembering the Dead in Glendalough

In ancient Irish monasteries, the dead were buried within the enclosure. Even though Glendalough, its sacred buildings and all its lands were confiscated during the Penal Times, the graveyard remained in use.

Even when public ceremonies were banned, people came to remember their dead, and held a 'Patron' and a fair on St. Kevin's Feastday, June 3rd. Patrons and fairs attract everyone, the devout and the lapsed, the saint and the sinner. The Irish people had suffered greatly, both during the Penal Times and later during the Great Famine. Many were emotionally scarred. Many too had turned to drink. Fighting was commonplace. In the late 1800s the patron in Glendalough sometimes ended in a drunken brawl.

These were our ancestors. As we come to Glendalough to visit the sacred sites, to draw close to God, and to seek the intercession of St. Kevin and all the saints of Glendalough, we also remember all our dead back through these tough centuries - including those who 'had their problems'.

Eternal rest grant unto them O Lord.
Look not upon their sins but embrace them in Your eternal love.

Bless also, Lord, those who are still suffering because of the brokenness that has come down to them through the generations.
Help us to bring Your love and compassion to broken people today.

Praying inside the Priests' House

Called the Priests' House when priests were later buried there.

In 789 the relics of St. Kevin were first enshrined in Glendalough.

The 'Priests' House' may have been built in the time of St. Laurence O Toole to give them greater dignity, while some suggest that it also served as a mortuary chapel.

It became a special place of prayer for pilgrims. When it was locked, the pilgrims stuck pieces of cloth in through the slit that served as a window to touch the sacred objects.

Many centuries later, with the monastery long gone, and every sacred site a prime spot to be buried, when two priests who had the gift of healing were buried in it in the 1700s, it once again became a place of special pilgrimage, with people even taking home the clay from their graves.

Today, not receiving as much attention from the tourists as the other sites, one may have the opportunity to sit inside it on the slab which may have been the base of an altar or a stand for the relics.

As you sit and pray, become aware that the Priests' House was most likely designed and blessed by St. Laurence O Toole, that it housed the relics of St. Kevin, and that holy priests were buried here.

A key element of the Glendalough pilgrimage is getting in touch with our Christian roots.

Most of the Irish dioceses originally centred around a monastic settlement, each of them with their own saints. As we get in touch emotionally and spiritually with St. Kevin, St. Laurence and the other saints who dedicated their lives to God in Glendalough, we will be able to go home and to have a sense of the sacred at our own local ancient Christian sites.

"For the sake of His sorrowful passion, and through the intercession of St. Kevin, St. Laurence and of all the saints of Glendalough, ... (insert intention)."

10

The Round Tower

The round tower is about 30 metres high. Think of the work that went into building it around 1,100 AD. The tower had seven floors, seven being a mystical number, a symbol of the victory of the Trinity (3) over the 4 cardinal points, north, south, east and west. It was also symbolic of fullness or completion. See P. 3 and P. 33 for more about seven's symbolism.

Round was also symbolic of completeness and of God's unending love. Thus we have the circular band or 'halo' around the focal point in Celtic crosses, the round enclosure around the monastic city, the round mound around St. Saviour's Church, and also the round caher or stone fort near the Upper Lake.

So a round tower of seven floors was as perfect a symbol of completeness and totality as one could get. It was in itself a powerful statement.

From the tower the call to prayer and to meals could be heard across the valley. (They had no watches.)

It also served as a place of refuge when under attack. Thus the entrance was about 3.5 metres up and could only be reached by ladder.

It served as a watch tower with four windows on the 7th floor, one facing in each of the 4 cardinal directions. This was both practical and symbolic. It was also an ideal place to store valuables.

The conical roof was destroyed by lightning in 1818, but was restored in 1876 using the original stones and a lightning conductor was put on top.

Lord, we think of the frantic prayers offered here by the monks when under attack, and of their resilience in picking up the pieces afterwards. Through their intercession, may we rise above the attacks that we suffer, and have the resilience to overcome setbacks.

St. Kevin's Church

St. Kevin's Church is popularly known as Kevin's Kitchen because of the chimney-like appearance of its little tower. Like the Round Tower, the tower of St. Kevin's Church has a window facing in each of the four cardinal directions. It served as the watch tower and the bell tower before the Round Tower was built and when the Round Tower was unmanned.

The roof of the Church has corbelled stones, which allows water to easily drain. When one includes the tower, this little Church originally had four storeys:- the main Church, a timber loft which served as living quarters, a small stone loft which gives strength to the roof, and the tower.

This gem of a Church, named after St. Kevin, was build sometime after 1100 AD, so several hundred years after St. Kevin, but possibly on the site of a much earlier Church. It still standing today, some 900 years later.

As it is not usually open and with tourists crowding all around, it may be difficult to pray a full decade here, but do offer at least a single prayer.

"For the sake of His sorrowful passion, and through the intercession of St. Kevin, ... (insert intention).

St. Kevin and St. Ciaran

Just outside the turnstile from St. Kevin's Church are the foundations of St. Ciaran's Church, excavated in 1875. St. Ciaran, (Kieran) was born in 512 AD. Just seven months after St. Ciaran founded the famous monastery at Clonmacnoise in 544, he died at the age of 33.

St. Ciaran's Church

The same thirst for God which led St. Kevin to seek solitude in Glendalough also led him to go on many pilgrimages - even as far as Rome. He also went on pilgrimage to Clonmacnoise (and other places).

In Clonmacnoise St. Kevin had a vision in which he saw St. Ciaran. This gave rise to the story that St. Ciaran had just died when Kevin arrived, but that he came alive to speak to Kevin. This story would only be credible if the date given for St. Kevin's death, 618 AD, is inaccurate. The legend that St. Kevin lived to be 120 should not be taken literally:- 120 was a symbolic number, a way of declaring that St. Kevin was the Moses of Glendalough. Ciaran was possibly dead even before Kevin was born.

Incidentally as recently as the 1970's, there were people who didn't know the year of their birth. The year given for St. Kevin's birth, 498, which was not written down for several hundred years after his death, is most likely very inaccurate. The year given for his death, 618, is more likely to be reasonable accurate. (One tradition lists it as 617.)

But even if St. Ciaran was long dead when St. Kevin arrived, Kevin almost certainly drew inspiration and ideas from his visit to Clonmacnoise. Clonmacnoise was already up and running as a monastic site, so visiting it, as well as making his own pilgrimage there, would have helped shape St. Kevin's plans for the monastic city in Glendalough.

While the more agile pilgrim will probably prefer to walk on, the less agile might sit on the low wall or possibly on the base of the altar of St. Ciaran's Church to pray a decade. You can just see the corner of the altar base in photo, in through the very narrow entrance to the sanctuary area.

Possible alternative wording for decade here
"For the sake of His sorrowful passion, and through the intercession of St. Kevin, St. Ciaran and all the saints of Ireland ...... (insert intention).

St. Mary's Church (Our Lady's Church)

Within a couple of hundred years, Glendalough had become a small city. Here religious and laity, celibate and married lived and worked. However there was also a degree of segregation - far more segregation indeed than some modern guides would have one believe. If, as some guides claim, there was then a married clergy, why have a separate women's church?

In fact within the monastic city, there was a double enclosure:- an inner sanctum for the monks, and an outer enclosure for the laity. The women's Church, and likely also a convent, was located not in the inner sanctum, but here, at a distance, in the outer enclosure.

St. Mary's is older than most of the other Glendalough Churches. One tradition has St. Kevin buried in St. Mary's but another tradition has him buried in Reefert Church and yet another tradition claims that the High Cross was erected at the spot of his burial.

To get to St. Mary's at the moment (2010), go up the main road and then enter over styles at a sheep shed 100 metres before the Youth Hostel. As few visit it, one usually has the freedom to pray aloud - or possibly even to offer the special Glendalough chaplet kneeling with arms outstretched like St. Kevin often prayed.

"For the sake of His sorrowful passion, and through the intercession of St. Kevin and of all the saints of Glendalough, ...(insert intention)."

The view from across the bridge on the Green Road

Glendalough Down The Centuries

In the Penal Times, all Church property in Glendalough was confiscated, and so it passed out of Catholic hands. People still came to Glendalough as pilgrims and prayed at the various sacred sites. But gradually the buildings, except for St. Kevin's Church and the Round Tower, fell into ruins.

In the early 1800s, the local priest, desiring once again to claim Glendalough for the Lord, and having no other chapel in the region, started to celebrate Mass in St. Kevin's Church on Sundays and Holydays. But sadly, after thirty years or so of tolerance, the Protestant minister stopped the celebration of Mass in St. Kevin's Church - even though the Catholics had no Church for miles around.

Part of the Glendalough experience is becoming aware of the anguish of our forefathers when their places of worship were taken from them and when Mass was banned.

Possible alternative wording for a decade as you walk on
For the sake of His sorrowful passion, and through the intercession of St. Kevin, help our youth to love the Mass.

15

The Green Road To The Upper Lake

When you cross the footbridge beyond St. Kevin's Church, you come out onto the Green Road at a spot known as the Deerstone from the old legend about St. Kevin receiving milk from a deer for a baby (See P 31.)

The Green Road is a picturesque ancient road that existed in monastic times, and possible even goes back to the time of the Druids.

If you turn right, it will take you up to the Upper Lake, Reefert Church and St. Kevin's Cell, a distance of just over a mile, so about a twenty minute walk for the average person. In monastic times the area between the two lakes was called the Eeshert, the name for a holy place around a hermitage in the wilderness. This is holy ground.

Did St. Kevin originally found the Monastic City and then use the Upper Lake as a place of retreat? Or did he begin at the Upper Lake and then start the Monastic City as the number of followers grew? The truth is we do not know. Yet this beautiful road is almost certainly built on an ancient path used by St. Kevin and by all the saints of Glendalough. They prayed as the walked. So too should we. Pray at least one decade along the way.

"For the sake of His sorrowful passion, and through the intercession of St. Kevin, ... (insert intention).

Reefert Church

Coming close to the Upper Lake, one comes to two footbridges. The first bridge leads to the waterfall. The second is on the spot of the ancient bridge to Reefert Church on one's left. The word Reefert comes from the Irish Righ Fearta "burial place of the kings."

The present Church dates from around 1050 AD, but it is almost certainly built on the site of the original church in which St. Kevin celebrated Mass. The fact that the kings chose it to be their burial site is an indication of the honour and reverence in which it was held.

There is a tradition that St. Kevin is buried here, but there is also a tradition that he is either buried at the site of the High Cross or in St. Mary's Church. Regardless, this is a most sacred spot. Enter it in a spirit of prayer.

Go to the sanctuary area in the Church. Become aware of all the Masses that were celebrated on this spot - including by St. Kevin himself.

Recite either the Gloria, the Holy Holy or the Our Father (aloud if there is no one else around) to unite yourself with all the Masses celebrated here. **Then, walking around inside the Church, offer a decade of the special Glendalough Chaplet.**

> **"For the sake of His sorrowful passion, and through the intercession of St. Kevin, ...** (insert intention).

The mound on which St. Kevin built his Beehive Cell.
Steps have been now inserted up to the cell so, if you are able to climb a stairs, you will be able to get to St. Kevin's Cell. One can just see the steps in photo.

The Path to St. Kevin's Cell

St. Kevin's Cell is on a hillside rocky mound just beyond Reefert Church, and over the Upper Lake. Those who are supple can leave the enclosure around Reefert Church by way of a style opposite the entrance then follow the path. Others have to go the long way around.

In this general area, his early followers also had their cells. They lived hard lives away from the comforts of the world. Despite the hardships, their total dedication to God attracted many more young men - and indeed young women too, and so the monastic city of Glendalough was born.

One is truly on sacred ground here, so one should make one's way from Reefert Church in a spirit of awe and prayer. Pray first that everyone who visits this area will be embraced in God's love.

Lord, embrace everyone who visits here in Your love.

Please pray a decade for your intentions as you climb to St. Kevin's Cell,

**"For the sake of His sorrowful passion, and through the intercession of St. Kevin and all the saints of Glendalough, ...
(insert intention)"**

18

St. Kevin's Cell

Only a few stones of the foundations of St. Kevin's cell survive, but it is thought to have been a "beehive" hut, called beehive because of its shape, like those still preserved on Skellig Michael, Co. Kerry. Once again one notices the round shape of the cell, round being a symbol of enclosure and of God's unending love.

Built in stone, and situated where the sun seldom reached, it would have been very cold.

This truly is one of the most sacred spots in Glendalough. Here St. Kevin lived a life of complete dedication to God and spent endless hours in prayer. Don't pass this sacred spot without praying.

The heart of Glendalough is taking time for God:- solitude, prayer, and perseverance in sacrifice and total dedication.

In all my visits to Glendalough over the past thirty years, I have always come here, and offered a decade of the chaplet, sitting on the stone when it is dry, or occasionally kneeling. It is good to lose one's embarrassment about praying in public, but never become an attention seeker.

One might also touch one's beads to the stones as a way of asking God to sanctify them. Then they will help you connect with St. Kevin and Glendalough when back home.

What is your number one intention? Cry it out to God here through the intercession of St. Kevin. Then pray at least one decade of the Glendalough chaplet here for that intention.

"For the sake of His sorrowful passion, and through the intercession of St. Kevin, ... (insert intention)"

Footnotes: - Whenever the cell is occupied, I find a spot nearby to sit and pray. The entire area is sanctified by St. Kevin and the other saints of Glendalough. Also, when I am in the cell and see others coming, I move on just as they arrive, praying as I walk, lest my presence deprive them of the opportunity of entering this sacred space.

St. Kevin's Bed

This is a man made cave about 30 feet (10 metres) up on the cliff face over the Upper Lake. It most likely was originally a Bronze Age grave. The cave is only about 3 foot high and 2.5 foot wide, though inside it widens to 4 feet, and is about 6 foot from front to back. Cutting it out was a time consuming and even dangerous undertaking - a sign of its importance.

It was used as a place for prayer and penance by St. Kevin, and later by St. Laurence O Toole amongst others. Even after St. Laurence became Archbishop of Dublin, he regularly came back to St. Kevin's bed and Glendalough during Lent.

If St. Kevin was born in 498 AD as claimed, (but which I consider highly unlikely,) this was just 66 years after St. Patrick came to Ireland. But even if St. Kevin wasn't born until perhaps 532 or even later, when one takes into account that the Druidic worship was not wiped out in its entirety overnight, when St. Kevin first came to Glendalough, this would have been a feared grave. St. Kevin sanctified it by sleeping in it - a very symbolic act for the native population.

In the past, it was a "must" for those making the pilgrimage to Glendalough. It was even very popular for newly married couples to go there on their wedding day. Given its size, if the bride and groom climbed in together, they truly became 'one flesh'!! But it can only be reached by boat, and sadly, due to insurance costs, the boats stopped going in 1965.

His bed is a reminder to us of the radical nature of the Glendalough pilgrimage as a place of prayer and for taking time alone for God.

Glendalough is a place where one should seek to go the extra mile in prayer, in fasting, in seeking solitude and in prayer walking. So please do pray an **occasional** decade as you walk,

"For the sake of His sorrowful passion, and through the intercession of St. Kevin, St. Laurence and all the saints of Glendalough (intention).

One can just see the outlines of the walls of Teampul na Skellig as one looks across the lake.

Teampul na Skellig

("The Church on the Rock". It was last renovated sometime around 1150, possibly by St. Laurence O Toole)

Teampul na Skellig is situated close to St. Kevin's bed on a tiny 'man levelled' bank on the far side of the Upper Lake. It is another powerful reminder that Glendalough is a place of solitude. Here for several hundred years, the most dedicated of the monks celebrated Mass in splendid solitude. They truly lived "life on the Rock"!

Most likely they were also fasting. It is a reminder to us of the tremendous awe they had for the Mass, and a challenge to us to develop a similar sense of awe and respect for what happens in Mass today, and for Jesus coming to us in Holy Communion.

"For the sake of His sorrowful passion, and through the intercession of St. Kevin and St. Laurence, grant us a deep sense of awe every time we receive Holy Communion"

Footnote:- Unlike St. Kevin's Bed, Teampul na Skellig can be reached by walking across the Glenealo River and then walking down the edge of the lake from the upper end.

But if doing so, do remember that this is a highly dangerous lake cut out of the valley by a glacier, with sheer drops to great depths. Swimming in the lake is highly dangerous. I have been to this site a couple of times, but never bother to do so nowadays. There are loads of sacred sites in Glendalough, and tremendous opportunities for solitude.

For those who are open, the entire valley is a sacred place.

Trinity Church

Trinity Church (not its original name) is located several hundred metres outside the monastic city beside the main road to Laragh. Its tower only fell in 1818 and the remains of its walls are in quite good condition.

It is said that St. Mochuarog founded this Church, or at least founded a Church on this site. St. Mochuarog is said to have come from Great Britain in St. Kevin's old age, and becoming a priest, he is said to have given St. Kevin the last sacraments just before Kevin's death.

Incidentally St. Kevin was succeeded as abbot by his nephew, St. Molibba, who became the first Bishop of Glendalough. Wherever one walks in Glendalough, one is walking on ground sanctified by saints.

Today one can easily enter Trinity Church over a style from the main road. As few people visit it, one will likely have the privacy to pray aloud or even to pray according to the manner of St. Kevin, kneeling with one's hands stretched sideways to form the shape of a cross.

"For the sake of His sorrowful passion, and through the intercession of St. Kevin, and all the saints of Glendalough ..... (insert intention).

St. Laurence O Toole

When Laurence was young, Dermot McMurrough, the infamous king of Leinster raided Laurence's father's lands and took Laurence as a hostage. Two years later, his father managed to get Dermot to hand Laurence over to the Bishop of Glendalough. In thanksgiving, his father asked the bishop to choose by lot one of his four sons to become a monk. Laurence replied, "No need for lots. It is my desire to dedicate my life to God in the service of the Church."

Such was his total dedication to God and his inspirational leadership, he was chosen as Abbot of Glendalough when only twenty five. He was invited to become Bishop of Glendalough when only twenty nine but declined on the basis of not having reached the required age.

Five years later, in 1162, he became the first Irish born Archbishop of Dublin where he immediately started implementing a programme of renewal despite much opposition. The Danish inhabitants of much of Dublin were at best nominally Christian.

Even as archbishop, he wore a hairshirt underneath his episcopal dress, lived a life of total prayer and austerity, and came back regularly for solitude to Glendalough, including sleeping in St. Kevin's bed and celebrating Mass in Teampul na Skellig.

The Green Road to St. Saviour's Church

Turn left at the Deerstone, and it is less than a mile to St. Saviour's Church.

Just as the upper half of the Green Road to St. Kevin's Cell was undoubtedly used by St. Kevin, this lower section was undoubtedly used repeatedly by St. Laurence (Lawrence) O Toole, (Lorcan O Tuathail) born 1128 died 1180.

All Glendalough is ground sanctified by saints.

"For the sake of His sorrowful passion, and through the intercession of St. Kevin, St. Laurence and all the saints of Glendalough, raise up young men and women who will dedicate their lives totally to You."

Looking down on St. Saviour's from the Green Road

St. Saviour's Monastery

As the monastic city grew, it became noisier and noisier, while the area around the Upper Lake had become a centre of religious trade and hospitality like a modern pilgrimage site. There were people everywhere. The solitude that had attracted St. Kevin to Glendalough was gone.

The Celtic monastery, with celibates and laity living in the same enclosure, had its advantages, but many truly dedicated monks desired more solitude. Meanwhile in Europe monks had their separate enclosures. People, like St. Laurence O Toole were attracted to the European model.

It was most likely St. Laurence, who continuously worked for reform first in Glendalough and later as Archbishop of Dublin, who established the monastery of the Augustinian Canons here almost a mile from the monastic city, with living quarters above and alongside the Church.

Note once again the almost circular shape of the surrounding mound despite the rectangular shape of the buildings:- the circle being a symbol of being encircled and enclosed in God's unending love.

St. Saviour's was for monks only. Here they dedicated their lives totally to God.

Lord, help us to dedicate our own lives to You.

Possible wording for decade on the way down to St. Saviour's,
"For the sake of His sorrowful passion, and through the intercession of St. Laurence, help us to dedicate our lives to you."

24

Interior of St. Saviour's Church
The newest Church in the valley, built possibly around 1160

As well as the fine Church, one can see the remnants of the living quarters on the left. A tiny stairs, recently blocked, used to lead up from the living quarters to further living quarters over the actual Church.

St. Saviour's was chosen as a place of solitude, quiet and prayer; a place to dedicate one's life totally to God. Today it is still a place of solitude with only a trickle of visitors. Thus it is an ideal place for spending some quiet time in prayer - or for praying with arms outstretched like St. Kevin.

Go to the sanctuary area of the Church. Become aware that on this spot, Jesus, working through St. Laurence and others, repeatedly transformed the bread and wine into His body and blood. To unite yourself with this, recite some prayer from the Mass, either the Gloria or the Our Father, or the Holy Holy. **"Lord, envelope me and every person who visits here with Your presence in this sacred spot."**

Invoking the reforming spirit of St. Laurence, a possible alternative wording for a decade of the Chaplet here would be,

"For the sake of His sorrowful passion, and through the intercession of St. Laurence, grant renewal in our church today."

Should there be other people in the Church, you could find a spot on the bank of the enclosure outside for a moment of quiet prayer and solitude.

Add a decade for your own intentions as you climb back to the Green Road.

St Kevin - A Man of God

It is said that when St. Cronan was baptising St. Kevin, he saw angels surrounding Kevin, and received a word of knowledge concerning Kevin's future. (St. Briege McKenna often gets images like this.)

As a teenager, Kevin studied at Kilnamanagh, (the cell of the monks) near Tallaght, founded by his uncle St. Eoghan, (Eugene), now patron saint of Derry. After some years he left the monastery, and crossed the mountains to live as a hermit in Glendalough. When reports reached his teachers of a young man performing miracles in Glendalough, they guessed who it was, and came and persuaded him to return to his studies.

Having been ordained priest by Bishop Lugidus, he left the monastery in Kilnamanagh. Some claim that he then established a religious settlement at Hollywood, (Holy Wood). In the past, Hollywood was also known as Killinkeyvin, from the Irish 'Cillin Chaoimhin' meaning 'Kevin's little Church'. However Killinkeyvin may have been established by St. Kevin later on as the staging point for pilgrims on their way to Glendalough.

By the time his lifestory was written 600 years later, the stories about how God guided him to return to Glendalough and the role of angels in this, had taken on fanciful dimensions, but you can be sure that he was guided by God, and that special things did happen. The story that St. Patrick later appeared to him is also totally credible.

St Kevin also suffered doubts. He was tempted to give up the entire venture in Glendalough. Then God gave him words of knowledge through other holy men, like St. Munna (Fintan) of Taghmon, to encourage him to persevere. This too is consistent with things I myself have seen happen.

Back then monks often knelt in prayer with their hands extended outwards so that their upper bodies took on the shape of a cross.
The next time you have a MAJOR special intention, pray the Glendalough Chaplet aloud in this position.
(Perhaps repeat daily for nine days.)

It appears that St. Kevin, who always went the extra mile in prayer, remained so still in this position that, on one occasion, a little bird perched on his hand - an incident guaranteed to make a good story. By the time the story came to be written six hundred years later, the claim was that he kept his hand extended for so long in prayer, that a blackbird laid her eggs in it, and that he didn't move his hand until the eggs were hatched.

St. Kevin And Celibacy

St. Kevin was born of a royal line of the tribe of Dal-Mesincorb. Even as a teenager he became a holy man, and clearly was a charismatic figure. Given all this, many ladies undoubtedly cast romantic eyes in his direction. Some, inspired by his example, sought to dedicate their own lives to God. But undoubtedly some desired only to possess him for themselves.

A story is told that when Kevin was either a student or a young priest in Kilnamanagh, a beautiful young lady called Kathleen wanted him for herself. She 'chased' him for some time without success, then growing more desperate, she sought him out when he was alone, and asked him directly to have sex with her.

It is one thing for a young man to live the celibate lifestyle when his celibacy is being respected. It is quite another thing to live it when an attractive young lady is asking him to have sex with her. Kevin was to become a great saint, but first he

Finding solitude in Glendalough today

was an ordinary full blooded young man with normal sexual desires.

It is said that, finding himself sexually aroused by her advances, he jumped into a clump of nestles semi naked - the 6th century equivalent of having a "cold shower". When Kathleen continued to pursue him, he plucked a bunch of the said nettles and began to beat her with them across her exposed parts. Some commentators refer to this as "violence". But I say, good for him! In fairness to her, instead of complaining, she got the message and repented. That was the real miracle.

Some commentators portray this incident as the "pushing away of human love". It was not!! It was the pushing away not of love but of lust; of sex being used not as an expression of love but out of a desire to possess.

By the time storytellers were finished with the story, they had St. Kevin throwing poor Kathleen to her death in the Upper Lake - despite the fact that the incident happened in Kilnamanagh and that she lived to convert! Meanwhile, if you have sexual struggles, invoke St. Kevin's assistance.

Lord Jesus, through the intercession of St. Kevin, bless and protect our priests and religious, and grant to us all an understanding of true love and deliverance from all sexual compulsions.

How St. Kevin Exorcised Glendalough

It is generally believed that "St. Kevin's Bed" was originally a Bronze Age tomb. Cutting that cave must have taken ages and even getting to it required a boat. Clearly some important person was buried there for mystical or religious reasons.

Then the original name for the Lower Lake was Lough na Peestha, the lake of the serpent. It was said to have had its own monster serpent. Given that this monster serpent was reputed to live in the Lower Lake, could "The Green Road" have existed prior to St. Kevin and been called after the Green Serpent God, after which Baltinglass (The Green Baal) at the other side of the Wicklow Mountains is also named. Green was a colour deeply associated with Druidic worship. Given that Baltinglass was a major centre of Druidic worship, it is quite likely that it was strong in Glendalough also.

Folklore told of a major struggle between St. Kevin and the serpent in the Lower Lake, with the serpent being a source of bad luck or of a curse (destroying his work and buildings) until St. Kevin caught and killed the serpent. This story is symbolic of St. Kevin delivering the valley from its pagan past and breaking whatever evil or curses that arose from its past.

Other stories have Kevin swimming in the lake, and standing for an hour praying in the lake daily while the serpent was still in it. Doing so would have been a powerful public witness by Kevin of his lack of fear of the serpent - and of the serpent god.

It is understandable that his swimming and praying in the lake, while the natives believed the serpent was still in it, would have caused them to have all sorts of images, including erotic images, of the serpent lapping itself around him. Hence the many such stories.

Just as his swimming and praying in the lake was a mighty statement that he feared neither the serpent nor the serpent god, so too St. Kevin's sleeping in the pagan burial chamber was a mighty statement that he feared neither the ancient pagan gods nor the spirits of the dead.

Possible wording for a decade of the chaplet
"For the sake of His sorrowful passion, and through the intercession of St. Kevin, may our homes (or X's home) **be delivered from all evil** (or from ...... {whatever evil you are concerned about})."

St. Kevin's Achievement

The first biography of St. Kevin was only written several hundred years after his death. By then the monastic city was at the height of its fame and glory, and the precise history of both St. Kevin and of the growth of the monastic settlement with its various Churches was long forgotten. But what was known was that it was St. Kevin's vision and total dedication to God that started it all. So it was all attributed to him.

Because of one man's total dedication to God, a great monastery had grown up which became a light not just to Ireland, but also to Europe which was then going through a very dark time. Glendalough together with Clonmacnoise and similar foundations helped make Ireland "the island of saints and scholars".

Glendalough became one of the four major pilgrimage places in Ireland, while priests who studied there went all over Europe.

Fourteen hundred years later, people are still being inspired and influenced by his life. How many thousands of people owe their conversion to the movement he started? It could even be millions!!

St. Kevin combined a life of radical asceticism with a capacity to inspire others. While he sought solitude in Glendalough, and to live in deep union with Jesus there, he did not cut himself off from the world. He went on pilgrimage to **Rome** which was then a truly mighty journey, bringing back relics for his foundation. This also meant that Glendalough operated in union with Rome.

He visited Clonmacnoise, and both visited St. Colmcille and was visited in Glendalough by St. Colmcille. He turned to St. Munna for advice when suffering doubts about his mission, while he studied under St. Eugene. So he was in close contact with the other Christian leaders of his time.

Such were the fruits of his work, that it is no wonder that the ancient writers, writing six hundred years after his death, had him living to be 120. In reality, if he crossed the Biblical old age of "three score and ten", he certainly had a strong constitution given his tough life.

But, because of his radical dedication to God, he has touched the lives of millions not just in Ireland but also abroad - a reminder to us that we too will make a difference if we are generous in our dedication to God.

Lord, may we too make the world a better place in which to live.

The Destruction of Glendalough

It is a sobering thought that it was at the time of its greatest material success that Glendalough was repeatedly attacked and destroyed. In St. Kevin's time, there was nothing there to plunder!

In 983, the monastic lands were plundered by the native Irish. In 984 the city was destroyed by the Danes. In 985 it was again destroyed by the Danes. In 1012 it was again burned by the Danes. In 1016, it was again burned by the Danes. It was again ravaged by the Danes a further 7 times between 1017 and 1163.

The 1163 destruction was two years after St. Laurence became Archbishop of Dublin - and Dublin was a Danish stronghold. Think of the level of union with God, who is love, that St. Laurence must have had to

Returning from the Upper Lake along the Green Road to the Monastic Village.

succeed in ministering to his Danish flock.

In 1176, it was ravaged by the Normans. In 1177, there was a great flood in the valley with St. Saviour's monastery fully swamped. In 1214, the diocese of Glendalough was amalgamated into the Dublin diocese - a real disaster both for Glendalough and for Ireland.

In 1398 King Richard 11 plundered, burned, and destroyed everything he could. Even though it lingered on for another 140 years as a monastery, it never recovered, and was finally taken from the Catholics during the suppression of the monasteries between 1536 and 1541.

The fact that the diocese of Glendalough had been absorbed into the Dublin Diocese, meant that even when it became legally possible, there was no leader attached to Glendalough who had the power and the finance to reestablish the ancient monastic area as a Christian centre. We can only pray that we may be able to do our small part in making it possible.

"For the sake of His sorrowful passion, and through the intercession of St. Kevin and of all the saints of Glendalough, may Glendalough once again become a centre of faith and pilgrimage."

The Deerstone and Holy Wells

In ancient times, it was not uncommon for a baby to be abandoned at a monastery. In the basic conditions at Glendalough in St. Kevin's time, getting milk for such a baby could have been very challenging, and the source of much prayer. Perhaps on one occasion "God provided" in a special way. Perhaps Kevin had rescued an orphan doe and it had become a pet, and perhaps he milked it for the baby.

By the time the story was written six hundred years later, the claim was that a doe came daily and gave her milk into the Ballaun (bowl cut in a rock) in photo, known today as the Deerstone on the edge of the Green Road close to St. Kevin's Church.

During the Penal times, when Catholics were deprived not just of Holy Communion but even Holy Water, the rainwater that fell in such fonts took on a special significance, and was treated as very special Holy Water.

Holy Wells:- The practice of blessing wells goes back to St. Patrick who blessed a number of wells around Ireland. Originally there were two holy wells at Glendalough. The Eeshert well (hermitage well) was close to Reefert Church. A second well, near the Green Road, a short distance from the Monastic City, can still be see today - though it is only a hole in the ground. Some people tie pieces of cloth on a nearby tree to represent their intentions - a practice I find quite 'strange' but won't judge without having its origins explained.

In Penal times, holy wells, just like bullauns, took on a special importance. To a degree they replaced Holy Communion in people's desire to make contact with the sacred and to come under God's blessing.
Because of this the Holy Wells were also often attacked and destroyed, and this happened in Glendalough.

The Poulanass Waterfall:- Close to St. Kevin's Cell is the **Poulanass** Waterfall, (Pool an Easa - the pool of the waterfall) seen while in flood in the photo. One can be sure that St. Kevin stood at this point and was uplifted by its beauty. Nature undoubtedly spoke to his heart.

Being touched by nature is an authentic part of the Glendalough Pilgrimage experience.

31

St. Kevin and the Animals :- As one walks in the upper valley, one will often see the deer in the distance. Here they have come down to the cliffs over the Upper Lake during the snow, but I don't think they were quite expecting to meet me!! This region of Glendalough is now a National Park, so it is important to respect the animals and birds. When St. Kevin first came to Glendalough, deer and goats roamed the hills. That they accepted him and that he became their friend is clear from the many legends concerning St. Kevin and the animals.

Market Square Cross - While the High Cross is very plain, a much more elaborate 2 metres high cross once stood in the Market Square near the modern hotel. It is now on display in the Visitors Centre. It shows the figure of a cleric, most likely St. Kevin, standing beneath the figure of Jesus on the cross.

Burial place of the Kings:- Even before the O Tooles, the chieftains of the region, McColmaks, were buried at Reefert Church. One tombstone sadly since stolen or destroyed, read "Jesus Christ, Mile deach, feuch corp re M uiThuill" (See the resting place of King Ui Thuil who died in Jesus Christ, 1014.)

The oak trees of Glendalough:- Derrybawn, (Doire Ban), "the white oak wood" is on your left as you go up the valley. Camaderry (Ceim O Doire) "pass of the oak wood" is on your right. Clearly in monastic times, it was a place of oak trees. An effort is now being made to re-establish oak and other native species.

Rivers:- The river at the entrance to the monastery is called the Glendassan River coming from the Glendassan valley (Gleann na Sonn) "Glen of the natural ramparts), while the Glenealo flows down through the Glendalough valley and also joins the two lakes. They combine to flow into the Avonmore (Abhainn Mor) "big river"

Prayer Stations:- Pilgrims walked around this mound in prayer seven times.

The 'Caher' (**Round Fort**). Behind the Prayer Station in the photo are the remains of a round stone fort. It may have been a building to serve the pilgrims, and many other structures then existed in this area; or the stone fort may date back to pagan times.

When the Pilgrims Came Walking

Most of the original pilgrims followed literally in St. Kevin's footsteps by walking 30 km over the Wicklow mountains, either coming down the path from Camaderry Mountain close to the Upper Lake or taking the short cut down through the Glenealo Valley.

On arriving at the Upper Lake, they crossed the valley towards Reefert Church. Along the way, despite having just walked 30 km over the Wicklow Mountains, they walked seven times around special prayer stations, which consisted of a round mound with a cross on top. While some people try to tell us that walking around an object in prayer came from the Druids, in fact it is deeply Biblical. In Joshua 6:1ff, God told the priests to march in prayer around Jericho once daily for seven days, and on the seventh day to do so seven times.

Praying as one walks is a key element of the Glendalough pilgrimage. Today there are a whole range of walks to suit every pilgrim. Do use them to revive the ancient practice of prayer walking in Glendalough. It will enrich your relationship with God.

Prayer Walking in Glendalough

For hundreds of years pilgrims came walking to Glendalough, praying as they walked. Seven pilgrimages to Glendalough were considered equal to one pilgrimage to Rome, seven representing fullness or totality.

I have been prayer walking in Glendalough for over thirty years. **In walking, I combine prayer, relaxation and exercise.**

Glendalough is about extending oneself physically and spiritually. A good long prayer walk into the hills is one way.

Glendalough is about solitude. If you are not free to walk alone, cut out the chit chat - and do offer at least seven decades of the Glendalough chaplet in stages.

Glendalough is about fasting. St. Kevin often lived on the pickings of nature. St. Lawrence was also big into fasting. What I find helpful is to not have breakfast until I come down out of the hills around 3.00 in the afternoon, and then to just have some cereal in the car.

Carry a rosary ring or a single decade beads. A time comes when one's mind knows that, if there is the ring or a beads in one's finger, one is meant to be praying.

Get into the rhythm of praying as one walks. One doesn't have to be repeating mental prayers the whole way around - perhaps a few Glendalough chaplets and a rosary or other prayers that have special meaning for you. In between times, just be aware of God as you walk.

A time comes when one's spirit takes over the prayer. One finds that even when one's mind stops repeating formal prayers, expressions of love for Jesus keep rising from one's heart.

One will also find that one can pray best both when climbing and when one's legs are really tired. The steeper the climb, the briefer the words, so one might cut the prayer on the Hail Mary beads back to, **"For the sake of His sorrowful passion, ... (insert intention)"**. And on the really steep climb, no words at all. Just an opening of one's heart to God.

See following pages for special prayer walks

Prayer Walk One

For those who wish to stay on the level.

Having gone through the Monastic Village, go out by "Kevin's Kitchen", cross the footbridge, then turn right at the Deerstone up the Green Road. It is 1.5 km to Reefert Church and St. Kevin's Cell.

One can then cross the valley close to the Upper Lake, near the remains of the round stone fort, and the pilgrims' prayer stations. This is where the early pilgrims crossed the valley to Reefert Church after their 30 km walk over the mountains from Hollywood.

Then, if you have the energy, go up the Miners Road by the Upper Lake which is on the level for a further 1.5 kilometres. You can view across to St. Kevin's Bed and Teampul na Skellig on the far side of the lake.

At the end of the road, you can see the remaining ruins of the miners village.

For variety, on arriving back at the car park at the Upper Lake, one could return to the Monastic City by a boardwalk, (see photo on page 34), from just behind the toilets.

Coming back along the Miners Road By the Upper Lake

At the Monastic City one could continue along the Green Road down towards St. Saviour's Church. This section of pathway tends to be quieter and so more conducive to prayer.

In all there are about 5 km on the flat along beautiful pathways, so 10 km when one counts the return journey.

Do pray at least one Glendalough Chaplet as you walk.

Some may find it helpful to pray a decade at different locations rather than the entire chaplet at once. Others may offer the entire chaplet at once and then add further decades as the Spirit leads.

Praying As One Climbs

Prayer walk 1 is on the flat. Prayer walk 2 involves reasonable climbs. Prayer Walk 3 involves 600 steps up the side of the mountain. Prayer Walk 4 involves a long steep climb. Prayer walk 5 combines much of Prayer Walks 2 and 4, while Prayer Walk 6 leads to the heights in photo.

Praying as one climbs is easier - except where the climbing leaves one breathless. The climbing stimulates the brain and helps it to focus, so there is less danger of all sorts of silly distracting thoughts. Keep the words of prayer brief and in tune with one's breathing:- the quicker your breathing, the shorter the words. Do pray for specific intentions.

On the steeper climbs, on the Hail Mary beads pray **"For the sake of His sorrowful passion, ... intention.**
Where the climb is not so steep, **"For the sake of His sorrowful passion, and through the intercession of St. Kevin ... .intention.**

At other times just let words of prayer rise from your spirit, words like **"Jesus I love You"**.

Panoramic Views From Prayer Walk Six. One can see across the mountains for countless miles around, and look right down into the valleys.

Gradually your inner spirit will grow in its union with Jesus and in its expressions of love and intimacy for Him. It will develop a capacity to keep praying on its own, so that even when your mind turns to other thoughts, you will find words of love for Jesus just flowing from your heart. This is a sign that your eternal spirit, which will live on when your mortal body dies, has truly come alive within you. Wonderful!!

At yet other times, just be content to walk in God's presence even for quite a distance without the need for words - just like walking with any friend. Do allow your heart to be touched by the beauty of the scenery.

The View of the Upper Lake from route of Prayer Walk Two.
The deep and dangerous Upper Lake has a mystical quality all its own. Varying with the light, there is always something new about it.

Prayer Walk Two

A walk along smooth paths of approx. 8 km, lasting about 1.5 to 2 hours. Moderate climbs along the side of Derrybawn Mt.

Walking prayerfully through the monastic city, turn right up the Green Road. Continue on until you reach the two footbridges near the Upper Lake. Cross over the second bridge and visit Reefert Church on your left. Then follow the path to St. Kevin's Cell. Having prayed there, go up the steps, then continue up the main path. Turn left over another two footbridges, then continue straight on. (Follow the orange arrows). **After about half a mile there is a seat from which you will have the above view over the Upper Lake.**

Continue straight on along this main pathway. Eventually it will bring you back down to the Green Road below St. Saviour's Church close to Laragh. Turn left back up the Green Road, making an optional visit to St. Saviour's Church as you pass on your way back to the Monastic City.

Or one can make this walk in reverse, starting by turning left down the Green Road towards St. Saviour's.

Be A Peace Builder

As you look down on the sacred ruins, recall Romans 8:35-37:- "Who will separate us from the love of Christ? Will affliction, or distress, or persecution, or hunger, or nakedness, or peril or sword. Yet in all this we are conquerors, through him who has granted us His love."

St. Laurence O Toole was to see his beloved Glendalough pillaged and destroyed several times. But he never allowed this to come between him and God who is Love. Instead he worked tirelessly for peace and reconciliation, both between the warring Irish factions, and between the Irish and the English.

Looking down on the Monastic City from route of Prayer Walk 2.

When he was appointed Archbishop of Dublin, he worked tirelessly to convert to Jesus and to the ways of peace, the Danish population of Dublin who had attacked his beloved Glendalough so often.

It was while again on a peace mission to King Henry 11, who was then visiting Normandy, that St. Laurence became ill and died at Eu.

As well as his remarkable life, the great number of miracles through his intercession led to his canonisation just forty five years later. He was the first Irish saint to be canonised by the Church under the then new processes for canonisation which are basically still with us to this day.

Where do you desire to see reconciliation? Invoke his intercession.

Possible wording of decade of chaplet as you walk,
"For the sake of His sorrowful passion, and through the intercession of St. Laurence, help me to be a peacemaker."

Or
"For the sake of His sorrowful passion, and through the intercession of St. Laurence, grant that ... and ... may be reconciled."

Prayer Walk Three

About 8 km taking about 2 to 2.5 hours, very steep climb up 'stairs' to top of mountain over Upper Lake. Spectacular views.

Leaving the monastic city, turn right up the Green Road. Do visit and pause to pray in both Reefert Church and St. Kevin's Cell.

Then continue up the steps, then up the main path. **Take the first turn right.** (Follow the blue arrows.) Then watch for an entrance on your right into the trees by way of steps up railway sleepers.

These steps bring you right to the top of the mountain over the Upper Lake. It is quite a climb, guaranteed to speed up one's heartbeat. In climbing the steps a stick can be a help. The views from the top are quite magnificent, with a couple of special viewing points provided.

Continue on along the top until you come to a blue arrow pointing to a little path down through the trees. This path would be easy to miss. It is before one comes to the next climb after having walked the full distance of the Upper Lake below.

This little path, which can be mucky and slippy in wet weather, is only about 100 metres long, and brings one down to a main path.

Then turn left along this main path and it will bring you down by the little Poulanass waterfall behind Reefert Church.

Looking down the then snow covered steps that give easy access to the mountain over Upper Lake. There are over 600 steps.

I only recommend Prayer Walk Three to those who don't have the time or the energy to do Prayer Walk Four. Prayer Walk Four, (white arrows), continues right over the mountain to come down at the other side of the Upper Lake.

39

Prayer Walk Four

About 12 km taking about 2.5 to 3.5 hours. Truly spectacular views. Very steep climbs. Some rough terrain. (Follow White Arrows)

Going through the Monastic City, turn right towards the Upper Lake. Then cross the valley to go up the road by the Upper Lake. One can look across to St. Kevin's bed and Teampul na Skellig Church on the far bank.

Continue on up through the ruins of **the mining village**. There was commercial mining in this valley for lead, zinc and silver from the 1790s to 1957. At the peak of production, 2,000 miners were employed between here and the adjoining Glendassan Valley. Small scale mining also took place here in ancient times.

The path goes us through the remains of the miners' village along a stony trail

The path from here up the mountain is quite rough at first. One has to pick one's way over some rough stones for a short distance. For the person not used to walking, going up by this side is safer than coming down, and it is also easier on the knees. This is part of the reason why I suggest that the first time you do this walk, that you go up from this side and come down the timber steps at the other. The views are also more spectacular going in this direction.

Then follow the path up the mountain.
Do remember to pray at least a chaplet as you climb.

For much of the way, railway sleepers have been provided. These protect the mountain from erosion as well as making it easier for us walkers. Before the railway sleepers and stone paths were put down, one was guaranteed two wet feet on this walk - plus a possible fall. As one goes over the mountain, the views are truly spectacular. Allow your heart to be touched by them.
Then as one comes down at the other side, do go to St. Kevin's Cell and Reefert Church for prayer.

In The Footsteps Of The Early Pilgrims
Prayer Walk Four Continued

Having climbed up the valley, one can now cross the Glenealo River by this footbridge. I well remember when there was no bridge. Crossing the river then was quite exciting - especially when it was in flood!

If you take the bridge out of the picture, this is the first view that St. Kevin and later many of the early pilgrims had of Glendalough - at least those who took the short-cut down the Glenealo Valley.

The last stretch of their long walk was 30 km over the mountains from Hollywood, (then known as Killinkeyvin "Kevin's little church"), with just markers along the way. Such was the difficulty of the terrain that for the very first pilgrims, two pilgrimages to Glendalough were considered equal to one to either Rome or Jerusalem. However, when the regular pilgrims' path was more established, seven pilgrimages to Glendalough were considered necessary to be equal to one pilgrimage to Rome or Jerusalem, the number seven being symbolic of completeness.

The challenges faced first by St. Kevin and then by these early pilgrims inspires us to be willing to stretch ourselves in Glendalough, and to literally go the extra mile with the Lord.

"For the sake of His sorrowful passion, and through the intercession of St. Kevin, ... (Intention)."

41

Awe Inspiring Views
Prayer Walk Four Continued

As one reaches the top of the mountain, the views are heart lifting. Allow oneself to feel a sense of awe at the beauty of creation.

The mountain here is known as the Spinc (from the Irish, An Spinc, meaning pointed hill).

Today there is a boardwalk to take one right over the top, keeping one's feet dry. Before the railway sleepers were put down, one was guaranteed wet feet, and the occasional fall - but it was more memorable! A stick is still, however, a real asset when climbing. Where one goes down on the other side, they have provided over 600 timber steps using the railway sleepers. It surely is the highest 'stairs' that most of us will ever climb.

It was very different in the time of St. Kevin. And he didn't have climbing boots! It is said that St. Kevin went barefoot and wore only the roughest clothes. He lived mostly on berries, herbs and roots. So do keep your own attire and food simple while here on pilgrimage.

When you reach the bottom of the 'stairs', turn left, then left again, then left yet again to visit St. Kevin's Cell, the most sacred place in Glendalough. Let the awe that touched your heart at the amazing views above now touch your heart again. Then continue down to Reefert Church.

There are steep cliffs over the Upper Lake. A railing is provided at the more dangerous points, but it is no place for unsupervised children, or for messing or bravado.

Prayer Walk Five

About 15 km, taking three to four hours. An amalgamation of most of walks one and three.

Leaving the Monastic City turn left down the Green Road, possibly opting to pray as one passes the path down to St. Saviour's rather than going down. Then about a half mile below St. Saviour's take a sharp right.

Continue the gradual climb up the mountain. Very few go this way, so one may have the opportunity to pray aloud as one walks.

Follow the path right on, with the view over the monastic village, then the view over the Upper Lake. After crossing the footbridges as one descends towards the Upper Lake, turn right down the main path and turn in left down the steps to pray in St. Kevin's Cell.
Visiting St. Kevin's Cell is 'a must' on all prayer walks in Glendalough.

Then go back up where you just came down. Turn right opposite the footbridges, then right again in through the trees and up the 'stairs' to the top of the mountain. Continue along the path over the Upper Lake, then up another climb to come down at the other side of the Upper Lake.

"For the sake of His sorrowful passion, and through the intercession of St. Kevin, ... (intention)."

43

Prayer Walk Six

Around 17 km across varying surfaces, steep climbs, panoramic views, 3.75 hours to 4.5 hours; (or 14 km and 3 to 3. 5 hours if one opts for the shorter return route). (It is another 3 km shorter if one starts from Upper Lake). A stick is a real help.

Go from the Monastic City up the Green Road to Reefert Church, then on to St. Kevin's Cell. Then continue up the steps, then up the main path.

Turn left over the two foot bridges, then continue straight for about half a mile, then take the first right. Then follow the red arrows through the wood. For part of this walk, one is walking along the path known as the Wicklow Way, which is marked with a yellow arrow. See post with yellow arrow in photo. Continue through the woods following the red and yellow arrows.

In the left of photo is a stake with a yellow arrow. The yellow arrow denotes the walk known as the Wicklow Way. Prayer Walk 6 includes about 3 miles of the Wicklow Way.

One can often walk for miles on Prayer Walk Six without meeting anyone. The path continues for about three miles through the wood, then when one exits the wood, the Wicklow Way (yellow arrow) continues on **whereas we turn right, (red arrow)**.

Then follow the path up the hill and turn right near the top to continue along a rough path. The views here are truly panoramic, but do also watch your step.

When you join the path over the Upper Lake, you have a choice. Turn right (red arrow) for the shorter way back over the Upper Lake and down the steps **OR** turn left (white arrow), and climb another peak to come down at the far side of the Upper Lake.

The longer form of this walk, at 17 km, is just over half the 30 km distance walked by the ancient pilgrims over the mountains, so it gives one a taste of the ancient Glendalough pilgrimage. It's my favourite walk!

Having One's Inner Spirit Come Alive

We have an eternal spirit that will live on when our mortal bodies die. This eternal spirit will then be able to see, to hear, to think and to feel without the need of a mortal body. (See my book, 'I want to go to Heaven the moment I die'.)

Here on earth, this eternal spirit is deep within us, conjoined to one's mortal body. It is the depths of our being, the most important part of who we are, but sadly it is often left malnourished.

One's eternal spirit is made for union with God. The person who does not have a living relationship with God is missing out.

At a certain stage in a person's spiritual journey, after one has come to a living relationship with Jesus, one's eternal spirit comes alive within one in a very special way. This is a truly beautiful experience - one of the most amazing experiences that a person can ever have. It is also a key element in what Jesus called Baptism in the Spirit, which in reality is one's inner spirit being so enveloped in God's love that it comes alive within the depths of one's being.

A section of the path along Prayer Walk 6 covered in a full foot of snow

One's eternal spirit then starts to operate on auto pilot, and one will often have the beautiful experience of words of prayer rising from deep within one's being without any need for one's mind to be involved. This wonderful experience of intimacy with Jesus, needs however to be both stimulated and nourished through a regular prayer life. Prayer walks in places like Glendalough can be a great help in this.

Lord Jesus, lead me into a deep personal relationship with Yourself. O Holy Spirit flood my heart with Your love.

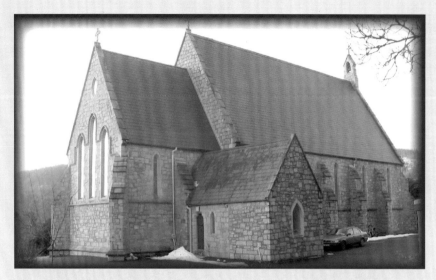

St. Kevin's Church, Glendalough

For three hundred years, Catholics had nowhere to celebrate Mass in Glendalough, and for part of that time, they risked death if they did celebrate it. In the early 1800s the practise of celebrating Mass in St. Kevin's Church in the Monastic City was resumed, but after thirty to forty years of tolerance, this was stopped by the then Protestant minister.

Thankfully a Captain Hugo, himself a Protestant, made a site available in 1847, and despite this being the time of the Great Famine in Ireland, through the generosity of two sponsors, Andrew Byrne and Peter Kelly, work was able to commence. The foundation stone was blessed on the feast of St. Kevin, June 3rd 1847 by Fr. Theobold Matthew, the apostle of temperance, and the present very fine Church was opened in 1850.

Built with beautiful granite stonework, it was restored to its original beauty in 2,000 to mark the Great Jubilee. There is a statue of St. Kevin, holding a blackbird, in the Church porch, while icons of St. Kevin and St. Lawrence O Toole were added for the Great Jubilee.

Its big drawback is that it is 2 km from the ancient Monastic City, and just off the main road to Glendalough so not even visible as one passes.

Recently five hermitages or Cillin for pilgrims were built in the Church grounds. See Glendalough Parish website for how to book one - and also for up-to-date Mass times.

God's Cottage, Glendalough

For 900 hundred years, life in Glendalough centred around prayer and living a life dedicated to God. Then around 1540, the monks were driven out and their lands confiscated. As I write this, 470 years later, Glendalough has more visitors than ever, but no official place for prayer at the ancient Monastic City.

I have often sat in St. Kevin's Cell and grieved for the fact that there was no Christian Centre beside the Monastic City. Then at Christmas 2009, I saw the "For Sale" sign on 'Peggy's Cottage' - and felt that it just had to be bought for the Lord - and become 'God's Cottage'.

Its only a tiny cottage, far from being the type of centre that I long to see, but it is beside the entrance to the Monastic City.

I prayed many 'Glendalough Chaplets', praying through the intercession of St. Kevin and all the saints of Glendalough, to be able to buy it for the Lord. Then after placing my first bid, I offered a nine day novena of 'Glendalough chaplets':- a chaplet in the morning praying with hands out like St. Kevin prayed, and a chaplet in the evening, prayer-walking. On the day after completing the nine day novena, I got the good news .

I bought it not for myself but for the Lord, so I am in the process of setting up a Trust with the intention of it being for the Lord until the end of time. It is merely a toe hold in Glendalough, but if the Lord blesses the venture, and with a Trust set up (**"God's Cottage Trust"**) for the express purpose of developing a wee Catholic centre beside the monastic buildings, perhaps the Lord will open new doors. (Meanwhile donations are appreciated.)

I am now praying (Feb. 2010) that, when the sale goes through, we will be able to get planning permission for the change of use to a "Christian Drop-in and Prayer Centre". If we get the permission, please God by 2011, we will be able to welcome visitors. For the latest news, and to see what we are in a position to offer visiting pilgrims at God's Cottage, see our website, www.**jesus**power**ministries.org** or just google either my name, Fr. Thaddeus Doyle, or The Curate's Diary.

Toilets, Meals, Parking, Masses, Info

Parking near the Monastic City is quite limited. The small car park alongside it is usually filled early in the day. There is a spacious car part at the Visitor's Centre just before one comes to the Monastic City.

There is a large car park by the Upper Lake, but there is a charge for parking here (€4 in 2010).

Toilets:- There are Public Toilets in the car park at the Upper Lake.

Food:- There is a fast food centre in the car park at the Upper Lake, a hotel beside the monastic city, a restaurant 3 km down the road, and another hotel in Laragh 4 km away.

Accommodation:- As well as the hotels, there are a range of B&Bs in the area including some by the road to the Upper Lake.

Public Toilets in car park at Upper Lake

Mass Times:- The modern St. Kevin's Church is located about a mile from the Monastic City just off the road to Laragh. See P. 46
At time of publication of this booklet, **January 2010**, the **Sunday Mass times** are Saturday 7.00 pm, Sundays 9.30 and 11.30 am. **Holydays** Vigil 7.00 pm, 9.30 am and 7.00 pm. Mon, Tues, Thurs, Frid 9.00 am; Wed 7.00 pm; First Friday 7.00 pm.

Do check the up-to-date times on the Glendalough Parish Website.

Hermitages:- Glendalough Parish has a number of hermitages. See Glendalough Parish Website.

God's Cottage Prayer Centre:- God's Cottage Christian Drop-in and Prayer Centre will hopefully open in 2011 just beside the entrance to the Monastic City. See P. 47. For up-to-date news on God's Cottage, see
www.**jesus**power**ministries**.org

Information:- As well as the Visitors Centre, there is an information centre in a cottage by the Green Road close to the Upper Lake.

Walks: I have listed a range of walks in this booklet. A fuller range of walks and maps are available from the Information Centre and the Visitors Centre. However if you follow the instructions for the walks in this booklet, you will be able to figure the rest out yourself.